THIS BOOK BELONGS TO

The Library of

....

....

©COPYRIGHT2023

ALL RIGHTS RESERVED

The content contained within this book may not be reproduced, duplicated, or transmitted without direct written permission from the author or the publisher. Under no circumstances will any blame or legal responsibility be held against the publisher, or author, for any damages, reparation, or monetary loss due to the information contained within this book. Either directly or indirectly.

Legal Notice:

This book is copyright protected. This book is only for personal use. You cannot amend, distribute, sell, use, quote, or paraphrase any part, or the content within this book, without the consent of the author or publisher.

Disclaimer Notice:

Please note the information contained within this document is for educational and entertainment purposes only. All effort has been executed to present accurate, up-to-date, and reliable, complete information. No warranties of any kind are declared or implied. Readers acknowledge that the author is not engaging in the rendering of legal, financial, medical, or professional advice. The content within this book has been derived from various sources. Please consult a licensed professional before attempting any techniques outlined in this book. By reading this document, the reader agrees that under no circumstances is the author responsible for any losses, direct or indirect, which are incurred as a result of the use of the information contained within this document, including, but not limited to — errors, omissions, or inaccuracies

I can't tell you how grateful I am that you decided to read my book. My most heartfelt thanks that you took time out of your life to choose my work and I hope you find benefit within these pages.

There are so many books available today that offer similar content so that makes it even more humbling that you decided to buying mine.

Tell me what you thought! I am eager to hear your opinion and ideas on what you read as are others who are looking for a good book to buy. Leave a review on Amazon.com so others can benefit from your wisdom!

With much thanks.

Table of Contents

SUMMARY — 6

Beginner's Guide to DIY Tambour Embroidery

   Chapter one — 26

      TAMBOUR BEADING ON EMBROIDERY FOR BEGINNERS — 26

   Chapter two — 43

      TAMBOUR LACE — 44

   Chapter three — 68

      Tambour beading — 68

SUMMARY

Welcome to the enchanting world of Tambour Embroidery! Prepare to be captivated by the intricate beauty and timeless elegance of this exquisite art form. Tambour Embroidery, also known as Luneville Embroidery, is a technique that originated in France in the 18th century and has since gained global recognition for its delicate and refined craftsmanship.

At its core, Tambour Embroidery involves the use of a specialized hook, known as a tambour hook, to create a series of chain stitches on a fabric stretched tightly in a frame. This technique allows for the creation of intricate designs and patterns, often featuring delicate beads, sequins, and threads. The result is a stunningly detailed and textured piece of art that showcases the skill and creativity of the embroiderer.

One of the defining characteristics of Tambour Embroidery is its versatility. This technique can be applied to a wide range of fabrics, including silk, tulle, and organza, allowing for endless possibilities in terms of design and texture. Whether it's a bridal gown adorned with shimmering beads or a delicate lace collar embellished with intricate motifs, Tambour Embroidery adds a touch of luxury and sophistication to any garment or accessory.

The art of Tambour Embroidery requires patience, precision, and a keen eye for detail. Each stitch must be carefully executed to ensure the desired effect, and the embroiderer must possess a deep understanding of the interplay between colors, textures, and materials. It is a labor-intensive process that demands dedication and skill, but the end result is truly breathtaking.

Tambour Embroidery has a rich history and has been embraced by cultures around the world. From the opulent gowns of the French court to the traditional garments of Indian brides, this technique has left its mark on fashion and design throughout the ages. Today, Tambour Embroidery continues to evolve and inspire contemporary designers, who incorporate its timeless beauty into their collections.

Whether you are a seasoned embroiderer or a novice eager to explore the world of needlework, Tambour Embroidery offers a unique and rewarding experience. It is a journey that allows you to connect with centuries of tradition and craftsmanship while expressing your own creativity and style. So, step into the world of Tambour Embroidery and let your imagination soar as you create stunning works of art that will be cherished for generations to come.

This response was truncated by the cut-off limit (max tokens). Open the sidebar, Increase the parameter in the settings and then regenerate.

Tambour embroidery is a highly intricate and delicate form of needlework that originated in France during the 18th century. The word "tambour" is derived from the French word for drum, which refers to the drum-like frame used in this technique. This embroidery style is characterized by the use of a hooked needle, known as a tambour hook, which is used to create a series of chain stitches on a fabric stretched tightly on the tambour frame.

The origins of tambour embroidery can be traced back to the Mughal Empire in India, where it was known as ""aari work."" This technique was brought to France by the wife of a French ambassador who was stationed in India. She was captivated by the intricate beauty of the embroidery and decided to introduce it to the French court. Tambour embroidery quickly gained popularity among the French aristocracy and became a highly sought-after skill.

The tambour hook used in this embroidery technique allows for quick and precise stitching, making it ideal for creating intricate designs and patterns. The fabric is stretched tightly on the tambour frame, providing a stable surface for the embroidery work. The tambour hook is inserted from the back of the fabric and brought up to the front, creating a loop. The hook is then inserted through the loop and pulled to create a chain stitch. This process is repeated continuously, resulting in a series of chain stitches that form the design.

Tambour embroidery is known for its versatility and can be used to embellish a wide range of fabrics, including silk, satin, and tulle. It is often used to create intricate motifs, floral patterns, and delicate lace-like designs. The use of metallic threads and beads is also common in tambour embroidery, adding a touch of glamour and opulence to the finished piece.

Over the years, tambour embroidery has evolved and adapted to different cultural influences. It has been incorporated into various traditional costumes and textiles, adding a touch of elegance and sophistication. Today, tambour embroidery continues to be practiced by skilled artisans and is highly valued for its intricate craftsmanship and timeless beauty. It is often seen in haute couture fashion, bridal wear, and luxury home decor.

In conclusion, tambour embroidery is a highly refined and intricate form of needlework that originated in France during the 18th century. Its origins can be traced back to the Mughal Empire in India, where it was known as "aari work."

Tambour embroidery is a beautiful and intricate form of embroidery that originated in France in the 18th century. It is characterized by its use of a specialized tambour hook, which is a small, pointed needle with a tiny hook at the end. This tool allows the embroiderer to create delicate and precise stitches, resulting in stunning and intricate designs.

In addition to the tambour hook, there are several other tools that are commonly used in tambour embroidery. One of these tools is the tambour frame, which is a circular or oval-shaped frame that holds the fabric taut while the embroidery is being done. The frame is typically made of wood or plastic and can be adjusted to accommodate different sizes of fabric.

Another important tool in tambour embroidery is the tambour handle. This is a small, handheld tool that is used to hold the tambour hook and guide it through the fabric. The handle is usually made of wood or plastic and is designed to be comfortable to hold and easy to maneuver.

In addition to these main tools, there are also several other accessories that can be used in tambour embroidery. One of these accessories is the tambour needle, which is a longer and thinner version of the tambour hook. The tambour needle is used for creating longer stitches and can be helpful for creating certain types of designs.

Another accessory that is commonly used in tambour embroidery is the tambour thread. This thread is typically made of a fine, smooth material such as silk or rayon, which allows it to glide easily through the fabric. The thread is available in a wide range of colors, allowing the embroiderer to create vibrant and colorful designs.

Finally, there are also several other tools and accessories that can be used in tambour embroidery, such as embroidery scissors, embroidery hoops, and embroidery transfer paper. These tools can be helpful for cutting thread, holding fabric in place, and transferring designs onto the fabric.

Overall, tambour embroidery tools are essential for creating beautiful and intricate designs. Whether you are a beginner or an experienced embroiderer, having the right tools can make a significant difference in the quality and precision of your work. So, if you are interested in trying tambour embroidery, make sure to invest in the necessary tools and accessories to get started on your creative journey.

The input is a request for a demonstration and practice of the foundation stitch. The foundation stitch is a fundamental stitch in various crafts such as knitting, crochet, and embroidery. It serves as the starting point for many projects and is essential for creating a strong and stable base.

To begin the demonstration, the instructor would first explain the purpose and importance of the foundation stitch. They would emphasize that mastering this stitch is crucial for achieving consistent tension and preventing any unraveling or distortion in the final piece.

Next, the instructor would demonstrate the step-by-step process of creating the foundation stitch. They would carefully explain each movement and technique involved, ensuring that the learners understand the proper hand positioning, yarn tension, and needle or hook manipulation.

During the demonstration, the instructor would also provide helpful tips and tricks to make the process easier and more efficient. They might suggest using a larger needle or hook size to make the stitches more visible and easier to work with, especially for beginners. Additionally, they might demonstrate different variations of the foundation stitch, such as the slip knot method or the chain stitch method, depending on the specific craft being taught.

After the demonstration, the learners would be given the opportunity to practice the foundation stitch themselves. The instructor would provide individual guidance and support, addressing any questions or difficulties that arise. They would encourage the learners to take their time and focus on achieving even tension and consistent stitch size.

To ensure a comprehensive understanding of the foundation stitch, the instructor might also provide examples of common mistakes or pitfalls to avoid. They would explain how to recognize and correct these errors, emphasizing the importance of patience and practice in mastering this essential skill.

Throughout the practice session, the instructor would provide constructive feedback and encouragement to motivate the learners. They would emphasize that mistakes are a natural part of the learning process and that with time and practice, the foundation stitch will become second nature.

In conclusion, the output of the demonstration and practice of the foundation stitch would be a thorough understanding and proficiency in this essential stitch. The learners would have gained the knowledge and skills necessary to confidently incorporate the foundation stitch into their future crafting projects.

When selecting a beginner-friendly Tambour pattern, there are several factors to consider. First and foremost, it is important to choose a pattern that is simple and easy to follow. Look for patterns that have clear instructions and minimal intricate details. This will help you grasp the basic techniques of Tambour embroidery without feeling overwhelmed.

Additionally, it is advisable to choose a pattern that uses basic stitches. As a beginner, you may not be familiar with complex stitches, so opting for patterns that utilize simple stitches such as chain stitch or backstitch can be beneficial. These stitches are relatively easy to learn and perfect for beginners to practice their skills.

Another aspect to consider when selecting a beginner-friendly Tambour pattern is the size of the design. It is recommended to start with smaller designs that do not require a significant amount of time and effort. This will allow you to complete the project in a reasonable timeframe and gain confidence in your abilities. As you progress and become more comfortable with Tambour embroidery, you can gradually move on to larger and more intricate designs.

Furthermore, it is helpful to choose a pattern that provides step-by-step instructions or even video tutorials. Visual aids can greatly assist beginners in understanding the techniques and processes involved in Tambour embroidery. Having access to clear and detailed instructions will ensure that you are able to follow along and execute the pattern correctly.

Lastly, consider the materials required for the pattern. As a beginner, it is advisable to choose patterns that require basic materials that are readily available. This will prevent you from having to invest in expensive or hard-to-find materials, allowing you to focus on learning and practicing the techniques instead.

In conclusion, when choosing a beginner-friendly Tambour pattern, prioritize simplicity, clear instructions, basic stitches, smaller designs, step-by-step guidance, and easily accessible materials. By considering these factors, you can select a pattern that is suitable for your skill level and embark on your Tambour embroidery journey with confidence."

This response was truncated by the cut-off limit (max tokens). Open the sidebar, Increase the parameter in the settings and then regenerate.

Common mistakes are errors or oversights that are frequently made by individuals in a particular activity or field. In the context of this input, we can assume that it refers to common mistakes made in various areas of life or work. These mistakes can range from simple errors in judgment to more complex issues that arise due to lack of knowledge or experience.

One common mistake that people often make is procrastination. Procrastination is the act of delaying or postponing tasks or activities, often resulting in unnecessary stress and a decrease in productivity. To avoid this mistake, individuals can implement effective time management techniques, such as creating a schedule or breaking tasks into smaller, more manageable parts. Additionally, setting clear goals and deadlines can help individuals stay motivated and focused on completing their tasks in a timely manner.

Another common mistake is poor communication. Communication is a vital skill in both personal and professional relationships, and misunderstandings or misinterpretations can lead to conflicts or inefficiencies. To avoid this mistake, individuals should strive to improve their communication skills by actively listening, asking clarifying questions, and being mindful of their non-verbal cues. Additionally, utilizing various communication tools and technologies, such as email or video conferencing, can help facilitate clear and effective communication, especially in remote or virtual work environments.

Lack of planning is yet another common mistake that individuals often make. Without proper planning, individuals may find themselves overwhelmed or unprepared for tasks or projects. To avoid this mistake, individuals should develop a habit of creating detailed plans and setting realistic goals. This includes identifying the necessary resources, establishing a timeline, and considering potential obstacles or challenges that may arise. Regularly reviewing and adjusting the plan as needed can also help individuals stay on track and ensure successful outcomes.

Furthermore, a common mistake that individuals make is failing to seek feedback or learn from their mistakes. Feedback is essential for personal and professional growth, as it provides valuable insights and perspectives that can help individuals improve their skills and performance. To avoid this mistake, individuals should actively seek feedback from trusted sources, such as mentors, colleagues, or supervisors. Additionally, reflecting on past mistakes and identifying areas for improvement can help individuals learn from their experiences and avoid repeating the same errors in the future.

In conclusion, common mistakes can hinder personal and professional growth, but they can be avoided with awareness and proactive measures.

This response was truncated by the cut-off limit (max tokens). Open the sidebar, Increase the parameter in the settings and then regenerate.

In this lesson, we will delve deeper into the world of tambour embroidery and explore additional stitches that can be used to create stunning designs. Tambour embroidery is a technique that involves creating intricate and delicate designs using a specialized tambour hook and a fabric stretched tightly in a hoop.

B. Overview of Tambour Embroidery

Before we dive into the additional tambour stitches, let's briefly recap the basics of tambour embroidery. Tambour embroidery originated in France in the 18th century and quickly gained popularity due to its ability to create intricate and delicate designs. The technique involves creating a series of chain stitches using a tambour hook, which is a small, pointed needle with a hook at the end. The fabric is stretched tightly in a hoop, and the hook is used to pull the thread through the fabric, creating a chain stitch. This technique allows for smooth and even stitches, making tambour embroidery perfect for creating intricate designs.

C. Introduction to Additional Tambour Stitches

Now that we have refreshed our memory on the basics of tambour embroidery, let's explore some additional stitches that can be used to enhance your designs.

1. Seed Stitch: The seed stitch is a simple yet effective stitch that can be used to fill in small areas or create texture in your designs. To create the seed stitch, simply insert the tambour hook into the fabric, pull the thread through, and then insert the hook back into the fabric close to the previous stitch, creating a small loop. Repeat this process to create a series of small loops, resembling seeds.

2. Satin Stitch: The satin stitch is a versatile stitch that can be used to fill in larger areas with smooth and even stitches. To create the satin stitch, insert the tambour hook into the fabric, pull the thread through, and then insert the hook back into the fabric close to the previous stitch,

creating a straight line. Repeat this process, slightly overlapping each stitch, until the desired area is filled.

3. Feather Stitch: The feather stitch is a decorative stitch that can be used to create flowing and organic designs. To create the feather stitch, insert the tambour hook into the fabric, pull the thread through, and then insert the hook back into the fabric slightly to the side of the previous stitch, creating a diagonal line. Repeat this process, alternating the direction of the stitches, to create a feather-like effect.

4. French Knot:

This response was truncated by the cut-off limit (max tokens). Open the sidebar, Increase the parameter in the settings and then regenerate.

Designing your own Tambour patterns can be a fun and creative process that allows you to personalize your embroidery projects. Whether you are a beginner or an experienced embroiderer, understanding the basics of designing Tambour patterns is essential to create unique and visually appealing designs.

To start designing your own Tambour patterns, it is important to have a clear idea of what you want to create. Consider the purpose of your embroidery project and the overall theme or style you want to achieve.

This will help you determine the motifs, colors, and overall composition of your design.

Next, gather inspiration from various sources such as nature, art, fashion, or even other embroidery designs. Look for patterns, shapes, and textures that catch your eye and resonate with your desired style. Take note of the elements that you find appealing and think about how you can incorporate them into your Tambour design.

Once you have gathered inspiration, it's time to sketch your design. Start by drawing the basic outline or shape of your motif on a piece of paper. This will serve as the foundation for your Tambour pattern. Experiment with different shapes, sizes, and arrangements to find the most visually pleasing composition.

After sketching the outline, add details and embellishments to your design. Consider using different stitches, such as chain stitch, satin stitch, or French knots, to create texture and depth. Play around with different thread colors and thicknesses to add visual interest to your design. Remember to keep in mind the overall theme or style you want to achieve and ensure that the details you add align with that vision.

Once you are satisfied with your sketch, transfer it onto your fabric. You can use a transfer pen or pencil to trace the design onto the fabric, or you can use a lightbox to trace the design directly onto the fabric. Make sure to transfer the design accurately and clearly, as this will serve as your guide when embroidering.

Now it's time to start embroidering your Tambour pattern. Thread your Tambour hook with the desired thread color and start stitching along the traced lines of your design. Use the Tambour hook to create chain stitches or other stitches that you have chosen for your design. Take your time and work carefully to ensure neat and even stitches.

As you progress with your embroidery, you may find that you want to make adjustments or add additional elements to your design.

There are several techniques that can be employed to secure and finish embroidery threads, ensuring that the final product is both visually appealing and durable. These techniques are essential in preventing the threads from unraveling or coming loose over time.

One commonly used technique is knotting the thread. This involves creating a small knot at the end of the thread before starting the embroidery. The knot should be tight enough to prevent the thread from slipping through the fabric, but not so tight that it distorts the surrounding stitches. Knotting is particularly useful when working with thicker threads or when starting a new section of embroidery.

Another technique is backstitching. This involves stitching over the previous stitches in the opposite direction, creating a secure line of stitches that reinforces the thread. Backstitching is especially useful when working with delicate or slippery fabrics, as it helps to anchor the thread in place.

In addition to knotting and backstitching, using a finishing knot can provide extra security. A finishing knot is created by passing the needle through the loop of the last stitch and pulling it tight. This creates a small knot at the end of the thread, preventing it from unraveling. Finishing knots are commonly used at the end of a section of embroidery or when changing thread colors.

To further secure the threads, some embroiderers use a technique called burying the thread. This involves weaving the thread through the back of the stitches, hiding it within the layers of fabric. Burying the thread not only ensures that it is securely held in place, but also creates a neater and more professional finish.

In addition to these techniques, using a quality thread and needle can greatly contribute to the overall security and durability of the embroidery. Choosing a thread that is appropriate for the fabric and project, as well as using a needle that is the correct size and sharpness, can help prevent the threads from breaking or coming loose.

Overall, securing and finishing embroidery threads is an important step in the embroidery process. By employing techniques such as knotting, backstitching, finishing knots, burying the thread, and using quality materials, embroiderers can ensure that their work remains intact and visually appealing for years to come.

This response was truncated by the cut-off limit (max tokens). Open the sidebar, Increase the parameter in the settings and then regenerate.

A. Tambour on unconventional surfaces refers to the technique of using a tambour needle to create embroidery or beadwork on surfaces that are not traditionally used for this purpose, such as wood, leather, or other unconventional materials. This technique allows for the creation of unique and visually striking designs that can add a touch of elegance and creativity to various objects and surfaces.

The tambour needle, also known as a tambour hook or tambour crochet hook, is a specialized tool used in tambour embroidery. It consists of a small, pointed hook attached to a handle, which allows for the easy manipulation of threads or beads. The technique involves creating a series of chain stitches or loops on the surface of the material, which can then be embellished with beads, sequins, or other decorative elements.

When working with unconventional surfaces, such as wood or leather, the process of tambour embroidery requires some modifications compared to traditional fabric-based embroidery. The surface needs to be prepared appropriately to ensure that the needle can easily penetrate the material without causing any damage. For example, when working on wood, it may be necessary to pre-drill small holes to guide the needle through the surface.

Chapter one
TAMBOUR BEADING ON EMBROIDERY FOR BEGINNERS

I'm going to focus on one approach in today's session that will allow you to achieve a couple of extremely useful things. It's a simple yet effective way to keep your work appearing neat and tidy.

It's not difficult to learn, and once you do, you'll discover a whole new universe of possibilities.

This approach, as far as I can determine, has no name, so I'll call it a "false stop" because that's exactly what it is: acting as if you've completed the task but actually continuing on.

Because my old lap hoop has broken off of its stand and I need to repair it, I photographed this tutorial in a little hoop attached to the edge of a table. If you can't afford a hoop with a stand right now, but you have other embroidery hoops on hand, this is an excellent solution.

Consider this adorable little flower that you've embroidered:

It's done, but there's no obvious path from the flower to the next section of your pattern. You could snip the thread, but who wants to weave in additional ends when they're done?! Not I.

Instead, you take the following simple steps:

To make a huge loop, pull out the last stitch on your needle. It doesn't have to be as large as the example.

Put your needle into the back of the work, directly adjacent to your last stitch, but not in the same cell as your last stitch if you're working on net. In other to tight the loop around the hook,

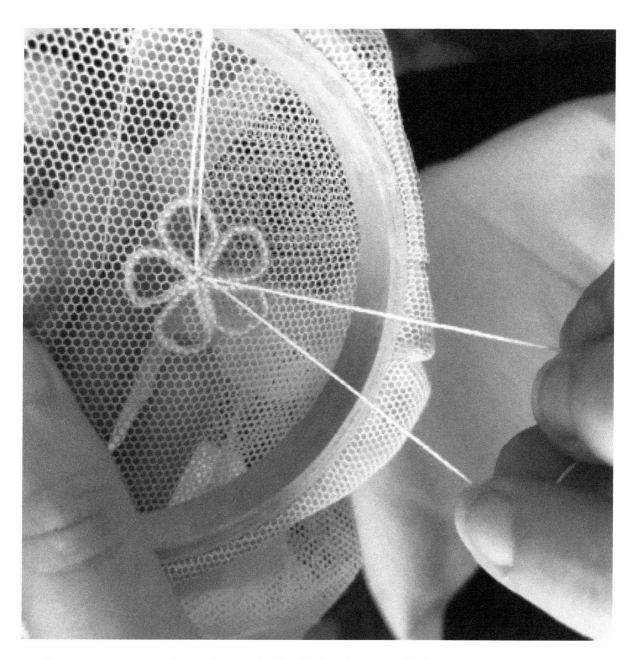

pull on your working thread. Pull the loop all the way to the back of the piece of art. This side will require a huge loop.

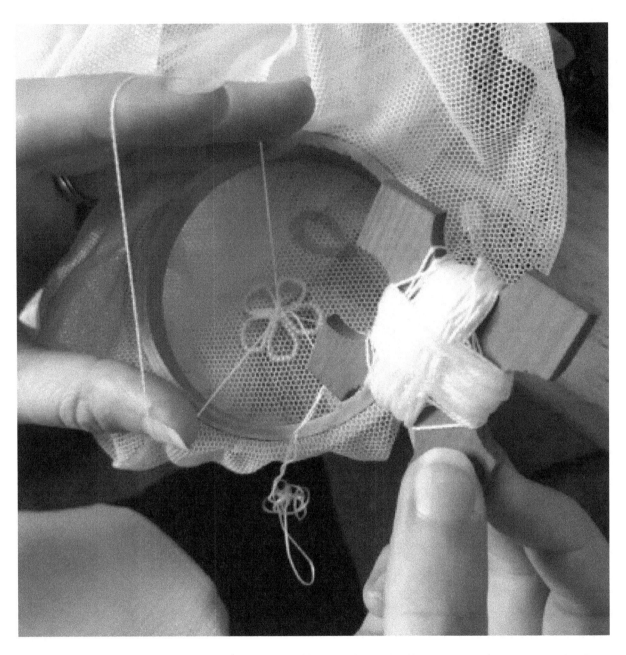

Take your needle and thread. Pass the full spool, thread winder, skein, or whatever you're working with through the loop.

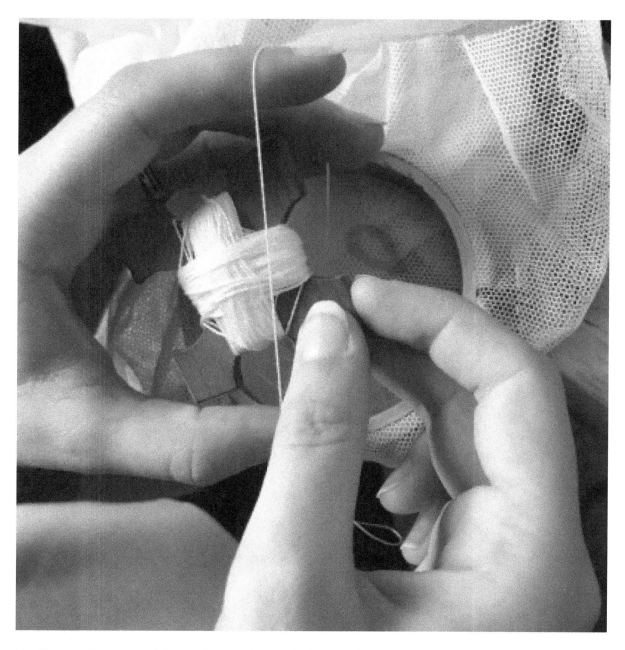

Pull on the working thread to tighten the loop around it. Continue tugging until the loop is completely tightened.

Pull only as much as you need to avoid distorting the stitches near the front of the work. The knot doesn't have to be really tight; it's only there to keep the work from pulling out while you move the working thread.

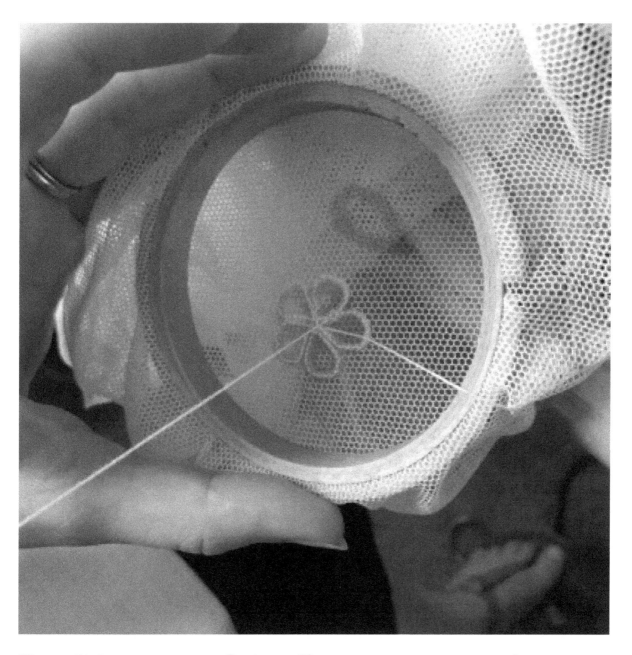

The stitches on your first motif are now secure, and you may continue working as usual by pulling up the working thread at another location in your design.

The working thread may plainly be seen going from place to place behind the fine muslin in this fragment from the Manchester Art Gallery.

Now that you've seen how a false stop can help you move your thread from one location to another without breaking it, I'll teach you how to use the same technique to turn acute corners.

Tambourine work does not like to go around corners, as you may have noticed. In order to make the turn, the turning stitch tends to deform and stick up. Fear not! This is avoidable.

Perform a false stop utilizing the identical techniques as above when you come to a point in your task where you need to turn a sharp corner.

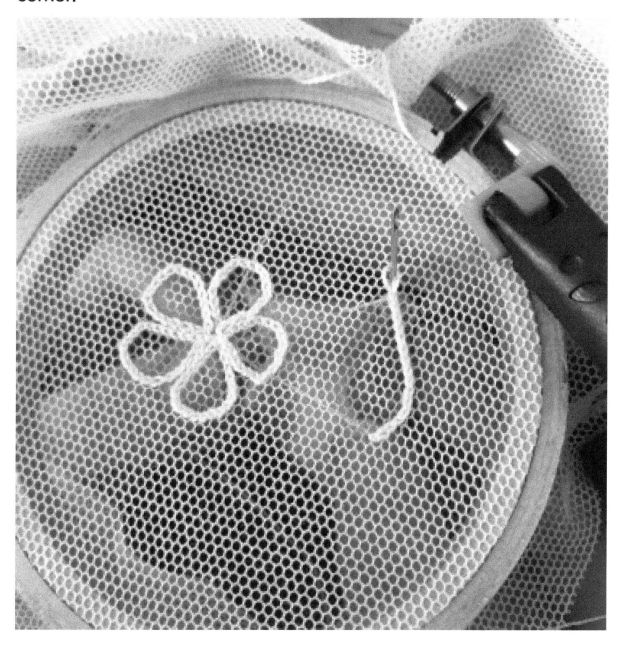

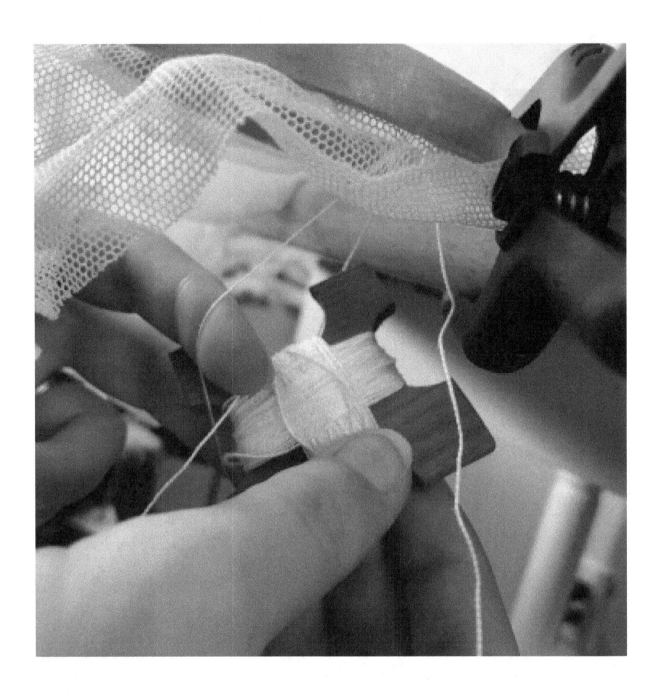

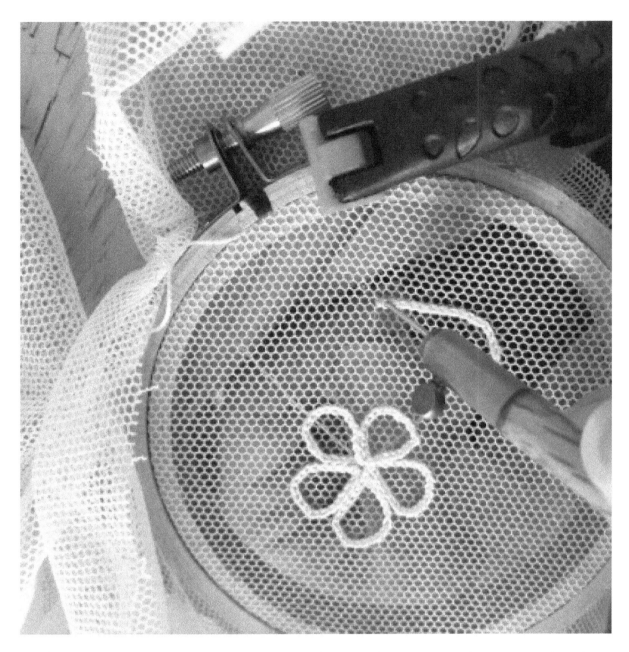

Instead of shifting to a new location, return your hook to the last stitch you finished—NOT the loop you pulled down as part of the false stop, but the fully visible thread before that. Raise the working thread.

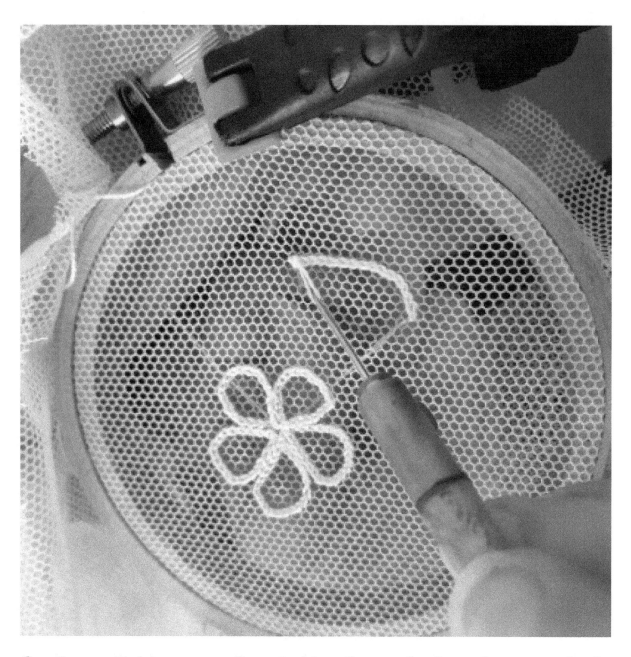

Continue stitching normally, admiring the perfection of your perfectly sharp corner.

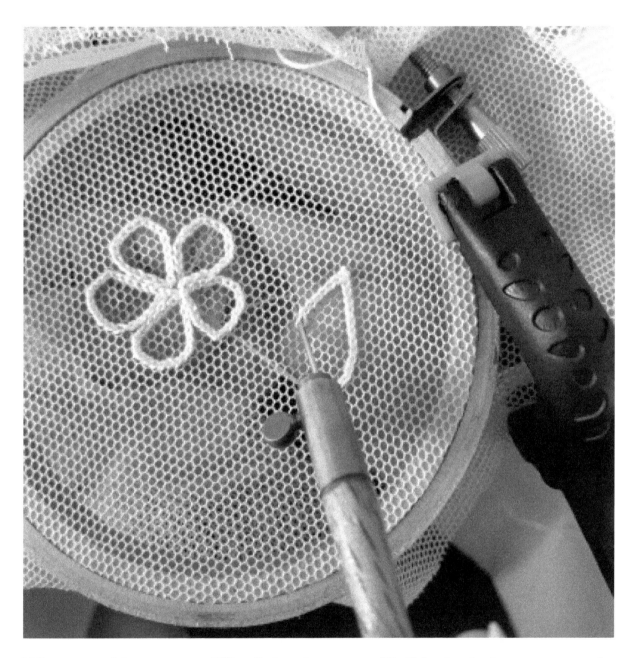

When working on a difficult tambour motif, this technique comes in helpful.

I hope you learn from this tutorial.

Chapter two

TAMBOUR LACE

Now that you know how to get started and complete the basic stitch, you can move on to embroidering something a little more interesting than straight lines. I'll start with something easy and straightforward. I just drew a little, softly curved vine with small, rounded leaves for this example. It's a motif that appears frequently in early nineteenth-century embroidery, therefore I've done a lot of it.

This design can be used to make a simple, elegant border for hems, ruffles, handkerchiefs, veils, sleeve cuffs, and just about anything else!

1st make a copy or create your design.

The first step is to have the design transferred onto our netting. This can be done in one of three ways.

1. Use a fabric marker that is water-soluble. I would have done this for this tutorial if I hadn't found a white one in my house, which would have been useless on my white cloth! This method is quick and easy to remove, but it's not ideal if you want to utilize the item as a period demonstration.

2. Using a pencil This procedure is very quick, so it's one of my favorites. Pencil is dark enough to see clearly while working, but it usually rubs off by the time a piece is finished, requiring just a fast wash to totally remove it. However, if you are concerned about being able to remove the markings, I would not recommend this for you.

3. Using the basting stitch This is the best way I've found, but it takes a lot longer and requires a lot more patience than the other two, so I typically dismiss it as too time-consuming. Simply use a needle and fine white thread to do a basting stitch around the motif. Because the tambour-work usually hides the basting entirely from the front, you can either pull it out or leave it in and trim the ends afterwards.

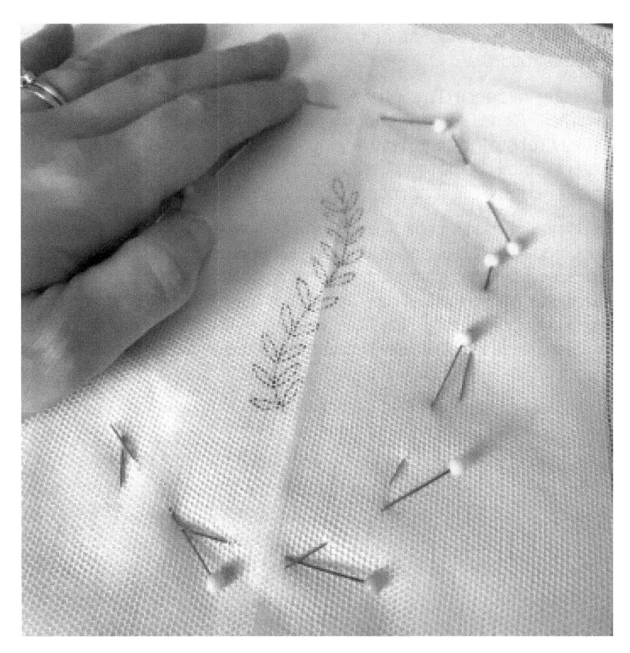

I begin by pinning the fabric down smoothly and securely over the design in either of these approaches. While copying, you want to make sure it moves as little as possible.

When the pencil is over the paper design, it appears to be alarmingly black, but much of that is just the drawing showing through. I like to start at the top left corner of the pattern and work my way down and to the right because I am right-handed. So, my hand doesn't smudge the pencil when I'm writing.

Step 2: Determine your route.

One of the most appealing features of tambour is how quickly it warms up. The ideal designs for this type of embroidery are those that can be worked in one continuous line, especially if you're just starting out. Even a complex design can be embroidered by a skilled embroiderer without ever cutting the thread. (In our next session, we'll go through how to skip from one part of a design to the next without breaking the thread or ripping out your previous stitches.)

Many designs are simple to figure out because you can see the path, you'll take just by looking at them, but if you're having problems, try replicating your basic design onto a piece of paper, potentially blown up larger, and working out the path there before you start stitching. It's quite frustrating to go halfway through a design just to realize you've made a mistake and are unable to proceed! More ends to weave in because you were forced to cut the thread prematurely is the last thing anyone wants.

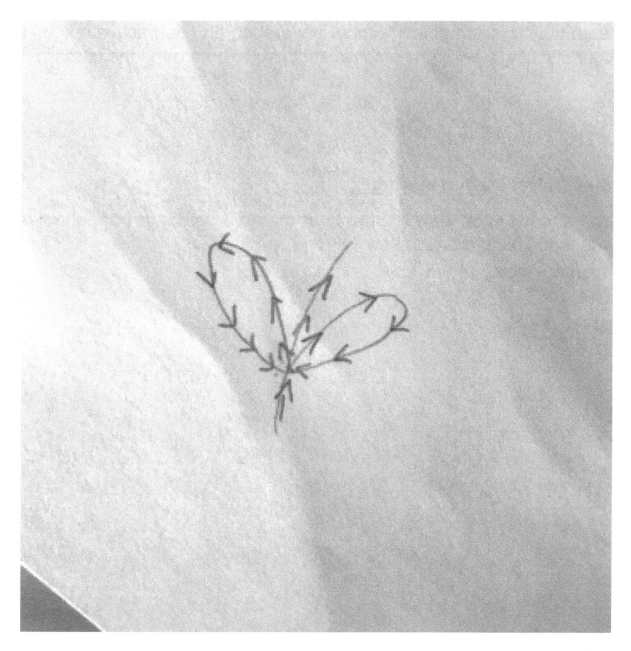

Each pair of leaves is worked together in a figure-eight pattern in this design. Up the stem, around the top of one leaf, around the top of the other leaf, and on up the stem. You might be tempted to work the leaves in a heart shape instead—over one leaf, around the bottoms of both, and back down the top of the second. If you do this, you will end up with a very sharp tip to deal with when you return up the stem from the top of the leaf. Sharp points should be avoided because they slow you down if used correctly. (In the following session, you'll learn how to stitch points without generating an unattractive bulge in your stitching where one stitch is straining to go around the corner.)

Step 3: Get started sewing!

You already know how to start your thread if you start from chapter one, and you're ready to sew.

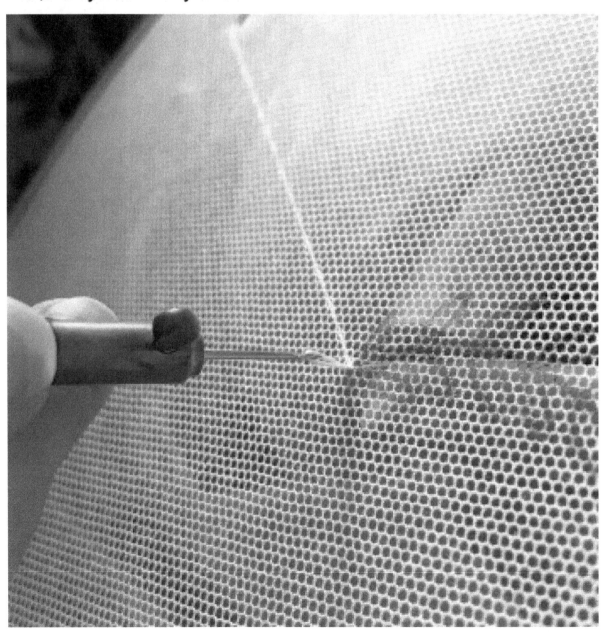

Bring your thread up to the stem's base.

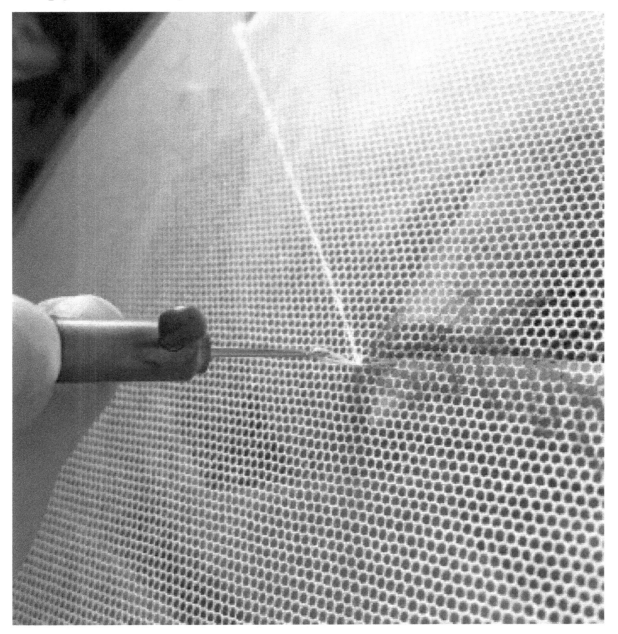

Begin working up and over the top of the first leaf with the basic stitch you learned in lesson one. It doesn't matter if you start with the left or right leaf, as long as you follow the pattern.

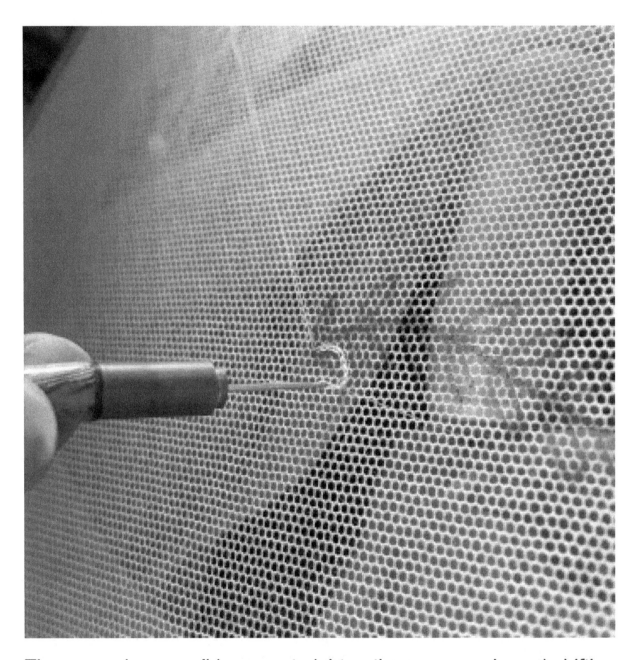

There may be no cell in your straight path as you work, and shifting to either side would disrupt the design. In this situation, you may need to skip a bar between two cells to reach the next available cell. These stitches will be slightly longer than the rest, but not by much that they will be noticeable in the design. Make sure you're not pulling the loops too tight or the fabric will pucker.

Continue along the leaf's bottom and up over the top of the leaf next to it. You should be able to stitch right over and into the same cell as your previous stitch where you cross the original stitching line. You don't want to fully skip over a cell because this would result in a longer stitch, which will detract from the work's beauty  and evenness.

Stitch along the bottom of your second leaf until you reach the point where all of the threads meet in the center.

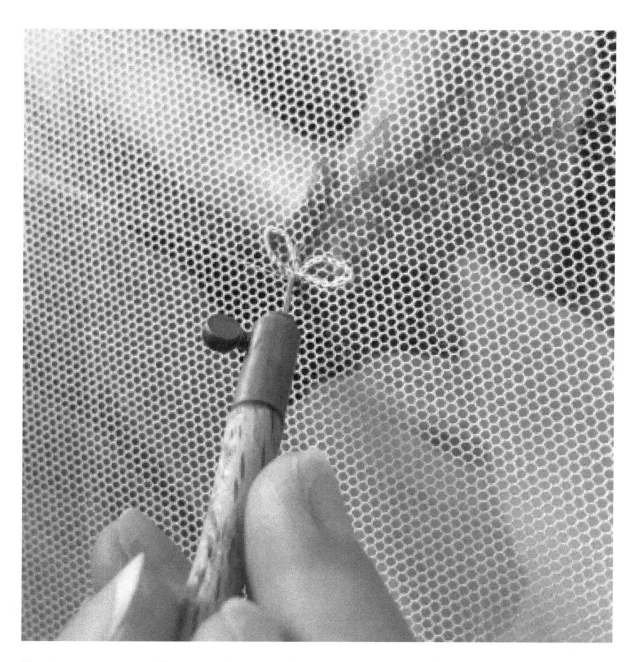

To keep your nice, uniform stitches and the design sharp, thread down through the point where all your lines of stitching meet. You won't be able to stitch in the same cell any longer, thus you'll have to go through the middle of your previous stitches. Move slowly and cautiously at first, and don't get irritated if your hook gets caught in the stitches as you bring the thread back through. Minute rotations of the hook are usually sufficient to locate a position where it can pass through. This section can be challenging, but the end effect will be far superior to skipping a stitch across the area.

Continue working the leaves up the stem as before. Insert your hook in the next cell that most closely matches your sketched design as you go. As you get acclimated to maneuvering around these minor curves, err towards the outer border of the pencil line if you're not sure where to go. Next time, we'll go over making sharp points once more! If there isn't a good cell to go to, skip a bar and stitch in the next accessible cell,

as previously. Rep this process till you reaches the final leaf.

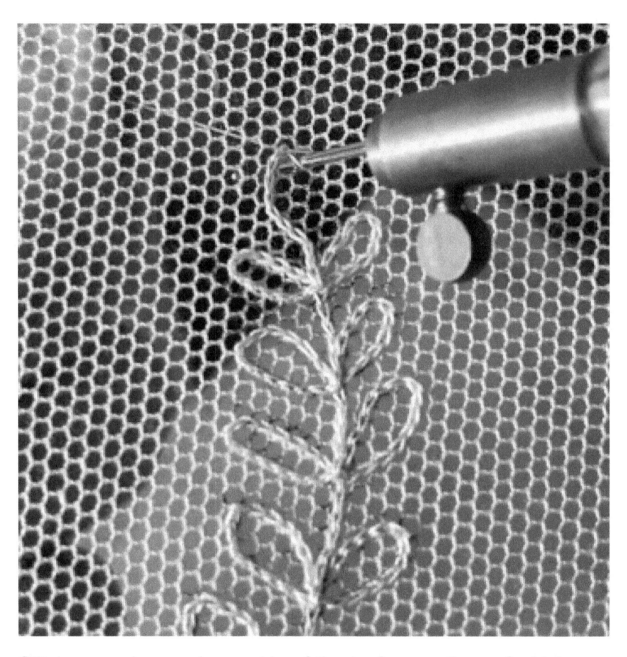

Stitch up and around one side of the leaf, regardless of which way you go.

Return to the place where the leaf joins the stem by turning around. Pull your thread out long and make your final stitch in the same cell as the end of the stem.

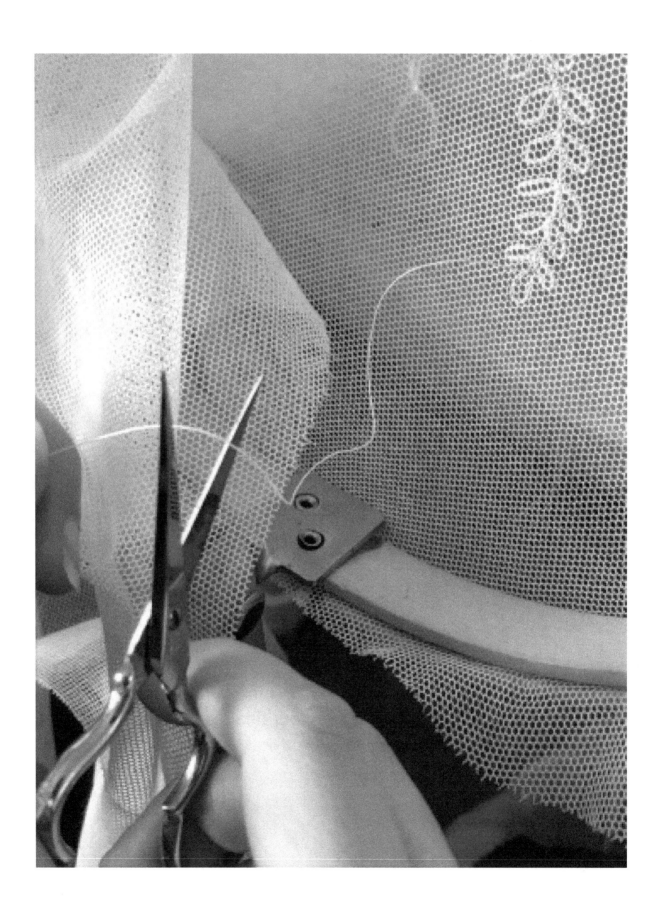

Clip the thread under your work, leaving a long enough tail to weave into the design's back. Don't pull on the thread while you're doing this! The last thing you want to do is take out your beautiful work before it's safe!

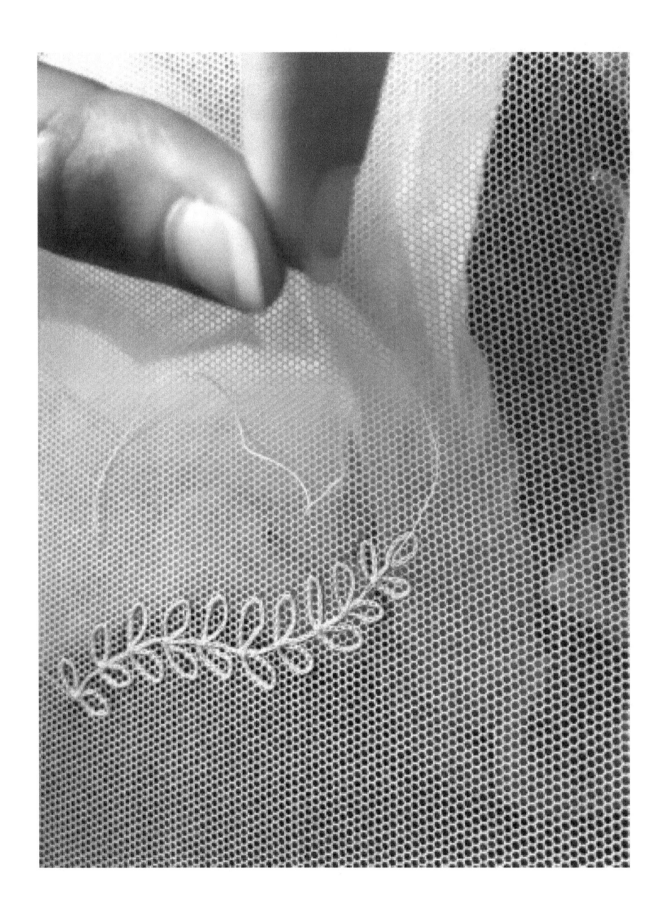

Pull the long thread loop back to the front of the work until the tail reaches the top.

Pull the thread tail back down through the same cell with your hook, but not through the last stitch you made.

That's all there is to it! Simply weave in your ends as instructed in Lesson

Chapter three
Tambour beading

Because there has been so much interest in my new Tambour project, I've decided to start posting somehow-toss! Because I won't be able to complete everything in one sitting, I'll be posting several classes over the following few weeks and months.

In these courses, I'll concentrate on lace because that's how I currently use tambour. I may expand this as I work on different projects, but all of the processes shown here are essentially the same for woven cloth work.

A little background: Tambour is a type of ornamentation that originated in or near India hundreds of years ago and moved to Europe in the mid-1700s when tambour embroidered textiles became popular. While tambour-work was initially all imported, it became a favorite activity for wealthy women by the late 18th century, and was especially popular as an adornment for the diaphanous garments of the 1790s and early 1800s. Tambour lace remained popular until the 1840s, when machine-made lace overtook it.

Check out this post by Two Nerdy History Girls for a more in-depth look at the history of tambour in Europe.

Today, I'll lead you through three fundamental steps:

1. Gathering materials and beginning the thread

2. The fundamental tambour stitch.

3. Bringing the thread to a close.

What you'll require:

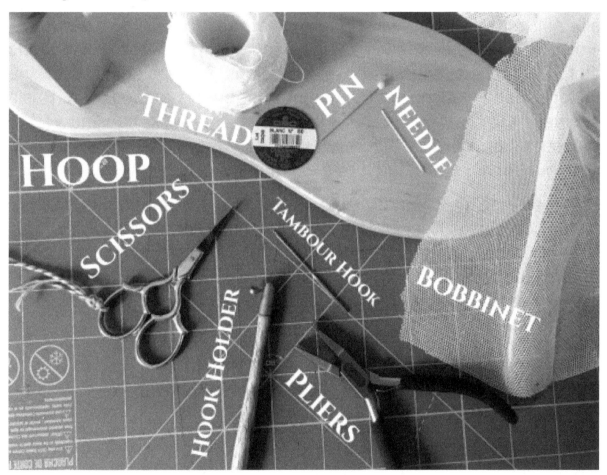

• An embroidery frame/hoop that stands alone. Professionals working on whole garment pieces utilize huge rectangular frames, while round ones are commonly seen in photographs of ladies creating tambour at home. Your sitting frame can be on the floor, at a table, or on your lap, but it must allow you to utilize both hands.

- A tambour hook/tambour needle—depending on your fabric and thread, these come in a variety of sizes. I assume the one I'm using in this video is a #90, but I'm not 100% sure because I put it in the holder a long time ago! There are varieties with and without a latch. I prefer not to use one, but if you have difficulties holding the thread without one, go ahead and try it!

- A hook holder—the wooden handle that keeps your hook in place as you work.

- Fabric—I usually work with lace on cotton bobbinet, but you can use silk net, muslin, linen, silk chiffon, or a variety of other materials. I wouldn't advocate working tambour on tulle from a regular fabric store. This isn't one of those occasions were starting with the cheapest and working your way up to the best is a good idea. Basic synthetic tulle is too thin and will catch on the hook, causing you to pull out all of your hair before you get very far. Please don't despise tambour because you had a bad experience with synthetic tulle!

- Thread—use any non-divisible thread (i.e. no embroidery floss). DMC Coordinate Special in size 70 is what I'm working with. This type of embroidery thread is wonderful because it has a good finish and makes crisp, substantial stitches. I use ordinary Gütermann 100 percent cotton sewing thread to fill in motifs when I need something really fine.

- Scissors

- A needle

- A pin

- A set of pliers can also be useful, but they are not required.

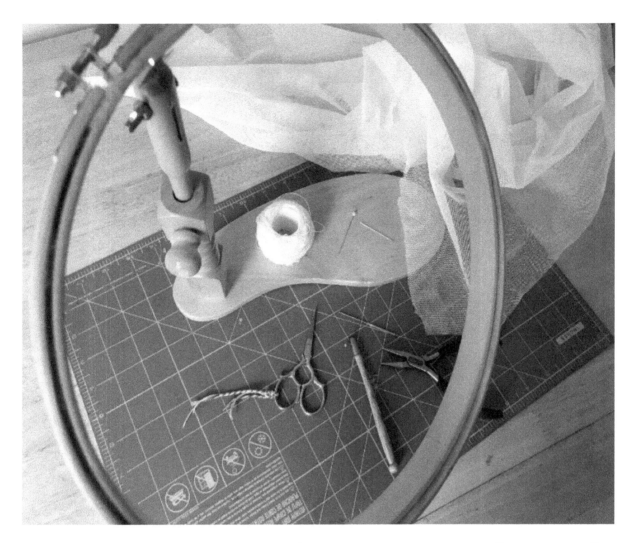

For my tools, I like to shop via the Lacis Museum's online store. On this page, you'll discover both a lap frame, like the one shown in this article, and a table-standing tambour frame. Hooks and holders can be found here. By Google the items, you can locate them in other places, however they're usually the identical products sold by various sellers.

Renaissance Fabrics, Mary Not Martha, and Originals by Kay are some of the places where I get my bobbinet.

You'll find a board of Tambour Resources on my Pinterest page, which I'll attempt to keep updated when I uncover new or interesting vendors. Please keep in mind that I may not have tried all of the items pinned there.

Step 1: Gather your supplies.

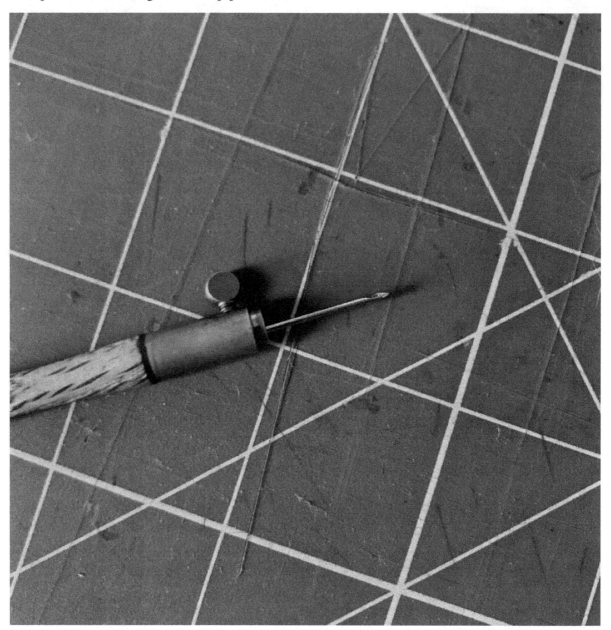

Tighten the screw on the hook into the hook holder. Keep the hook pointing in the same direction as the screw so you can always tell which way the hook is facing without looking at it. This is vital information. If you keep the hook short, it will be easier to manipulate. Mine is roughly 3/4" out of the holder.

Before you put your cloth in the hoop, you should transfer your design to it. I did not draw a design because I am only displaying the stitch at this time, but I will cover it in more detail in future tutorials on following a design. If I won't be displaying in period clothing while working on the designs, I mark them with a blue water-soluble fabric marker. (Before using your marker on a swatch of fabric, make sure it comes out.) Otherwise, I either write it in pencil, which usually rubs away to the point where it is unnoticeable by the time the project is finished, or I baste it in very fine white thread, which will be hidden by the finished work.

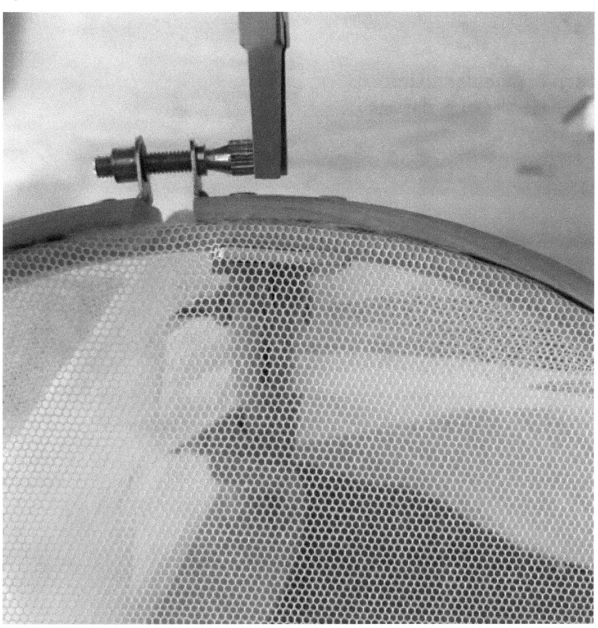

Place your fabric in the hoop. Tighten the screw just enough to keep everything in place, then pull the fabric taut and tighten the hoop even more. Repeat this process until the cloth is as taut as possible and the hoop screw will not tighten any more. I finish using a pair of pliers to ensure that it is as tight as possible. The name 'tambour' means 'drum,' and the fabric used in this art must be as tight as a drum head. This prevents puckering of the stitches once the fabric is removed from the hoop.

Step 2: Tighten the thread.

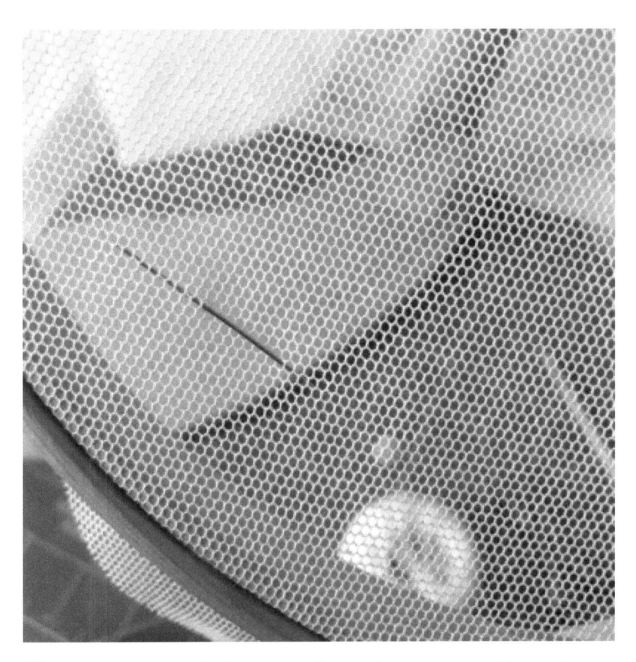

Place a pin several inches away from where you want to start your stitching on the underside of the cloth.

Wrap the end of your thread around the pin many times on the bottom of the fabric until it feels secure. Keep the thread's working end attached to the spool. If everything goes well in a tambour-work project, you won't have to cut the thread until the end.

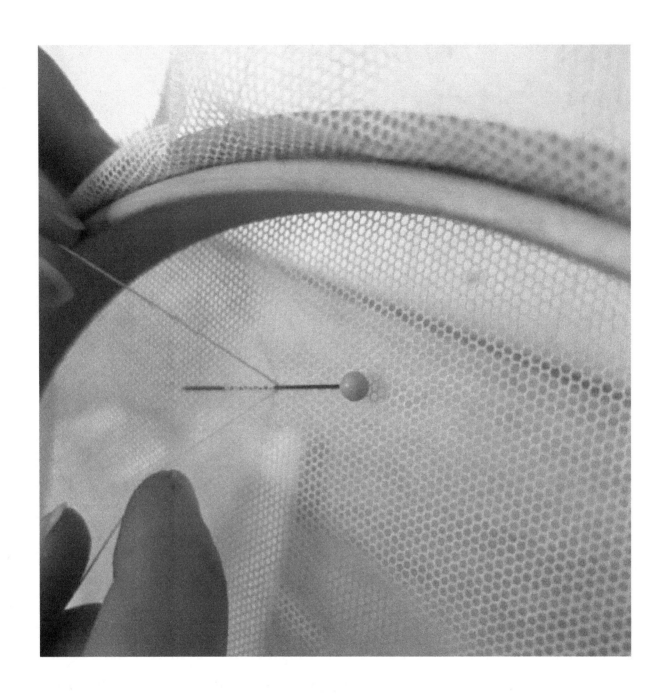

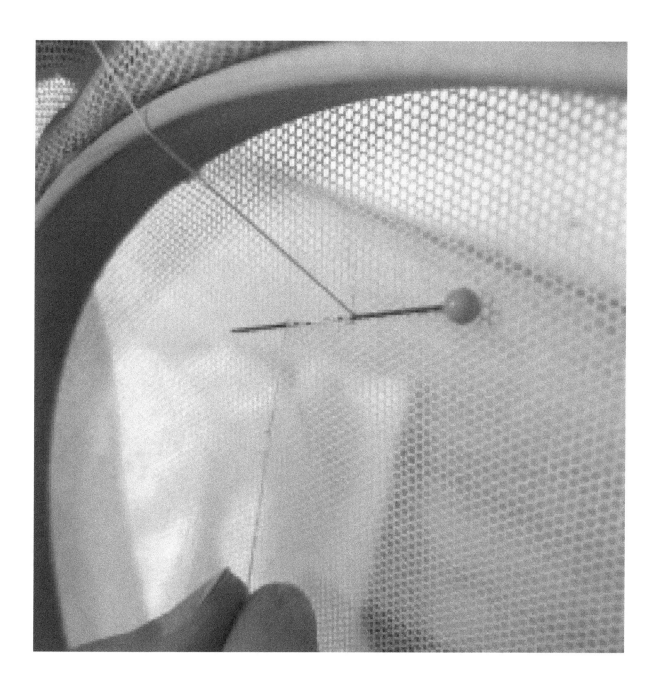

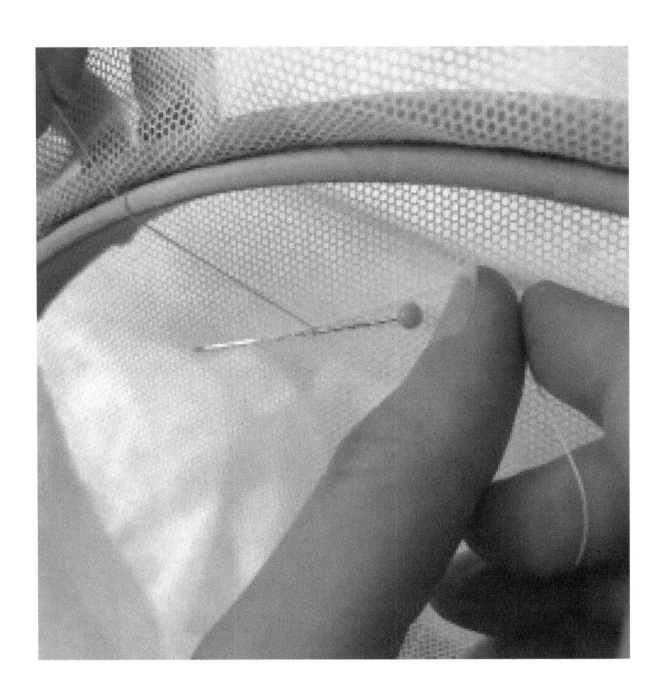

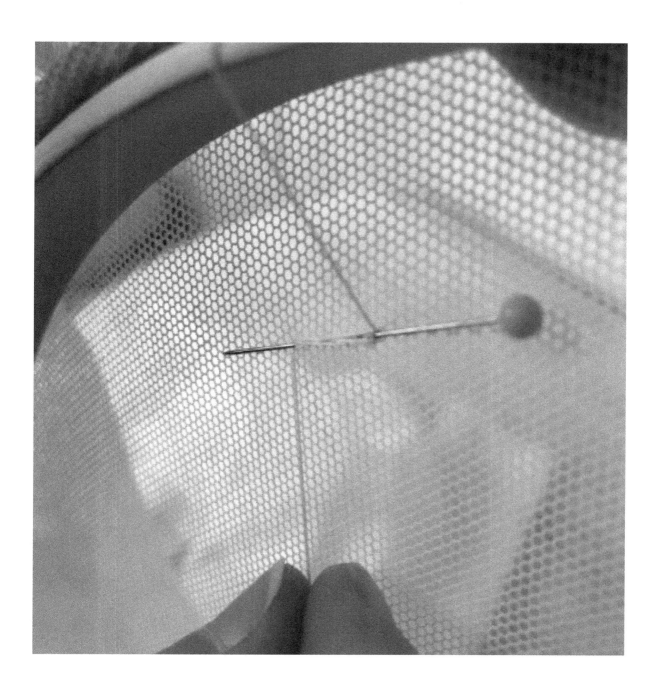

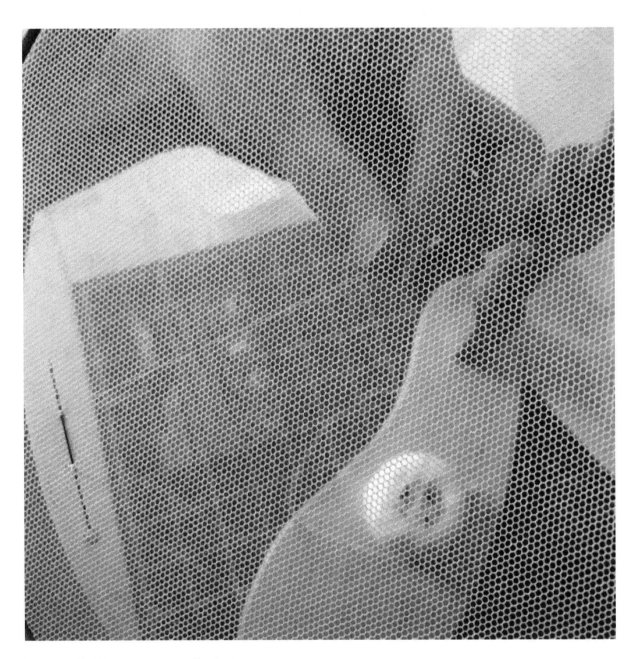

Step 3: The Basic Stitch

I recommend that you read through this step several times before attempting it on your own. It will be easier to avoid confusion if you have all of the facts in your brain before you begin.

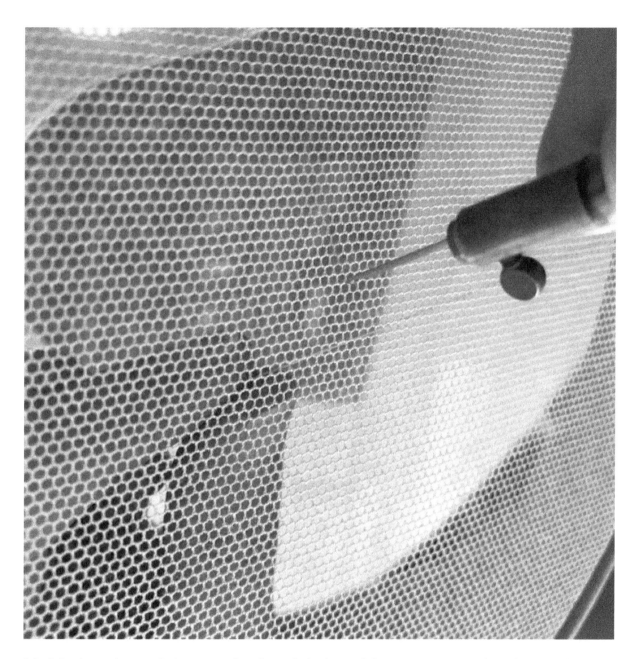

Hold the thread beneath the fabric with your non-dominant hand. Insert your hook through the fabric with your dominant hand. The hook should be pointed in the direction you want to go. Your fabric should be nearly perpendicular to the handle.

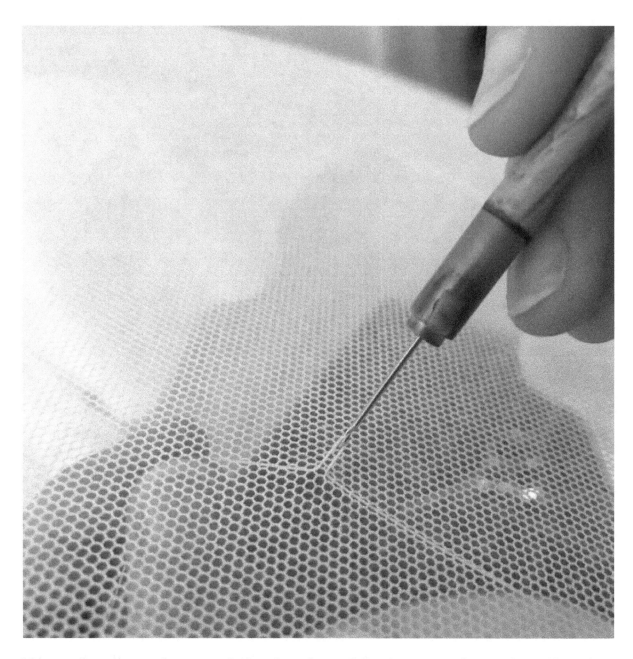

Wrap the thread around the hook, rotate it away from the direction you want your line of stitches to go (in this case, the hook is facing directly towards the camera, and I want to stitch along the line directly away from the camera), and pull up a loop of thread.

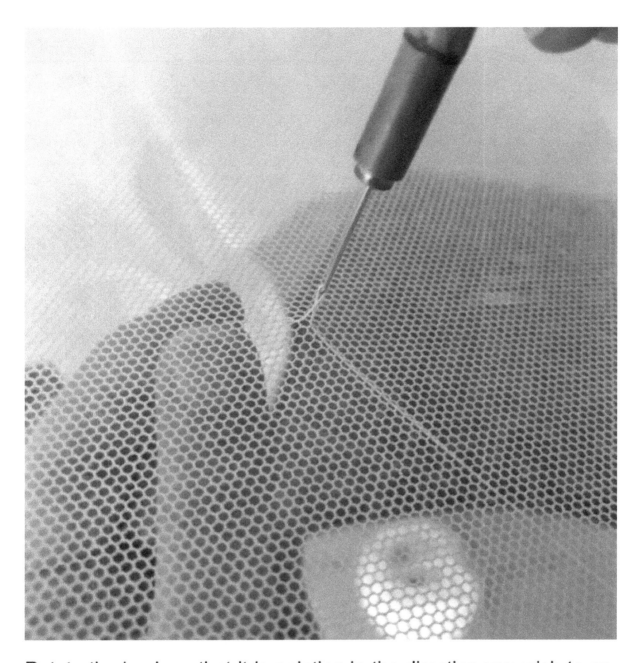

Rotate the hook so that it is pointing in the direction you wish to go. This keeps the thread securely in the hook as you go on to the next stitch.

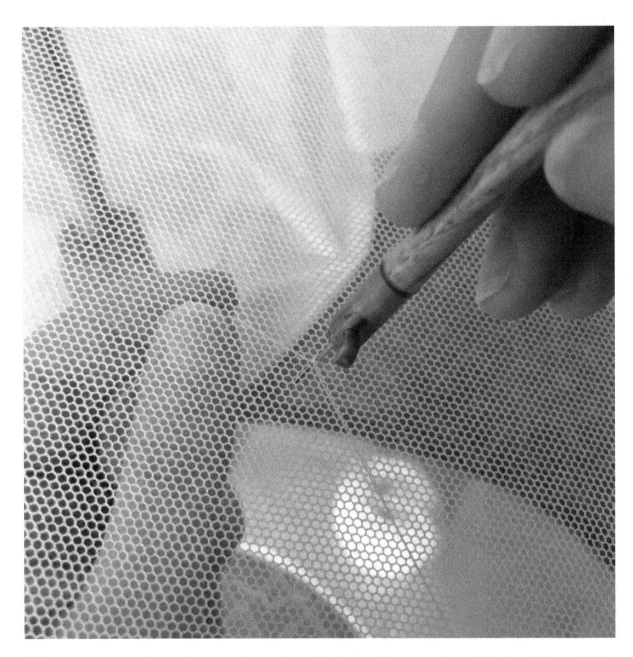

Place the hook in the next net cell along the embroidering line. This is the most difficult stitch, so don't worry if you drop it and have to restart a few times.

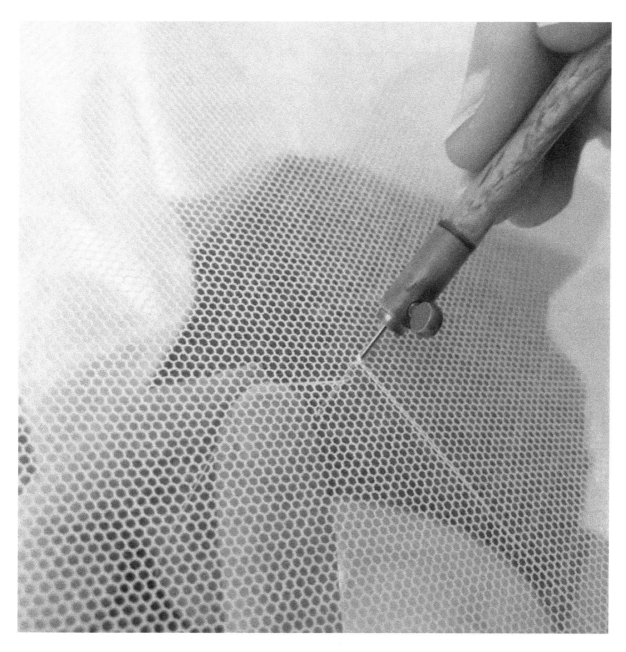

As you wrap the thread around the hook, rotate it away from your line of travel so that the thread catches in the hook as you bring it back up.

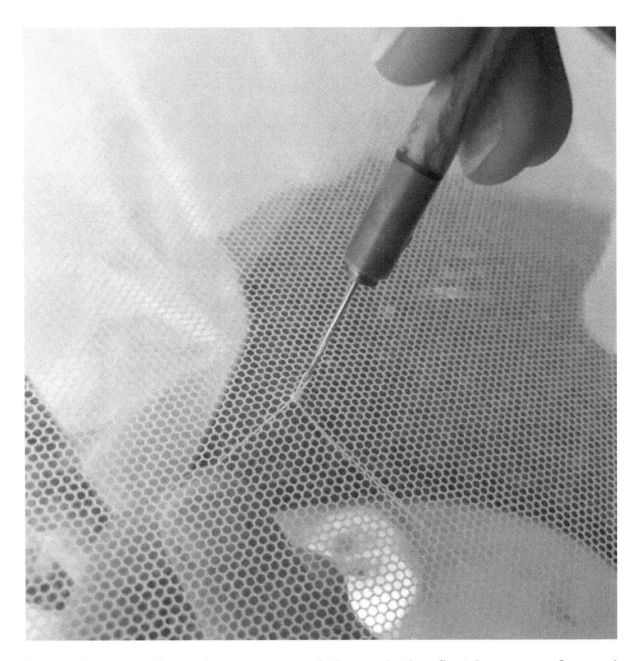

Bring the new thread wrap up and through the first loop you formed with the hook. When this happens, the hook must face away from your line of travel, towards the stitch you've already made. Instead of catching on the loop of the thread, the hook can travel through the point of the chain. You can also aid the hook's passage through the fabric by applying little pressure to the holder in the direction of movement, so that the hook's back is lightly pressed against the net. This will allow the hook to clear the fabric as much as possible without catching.

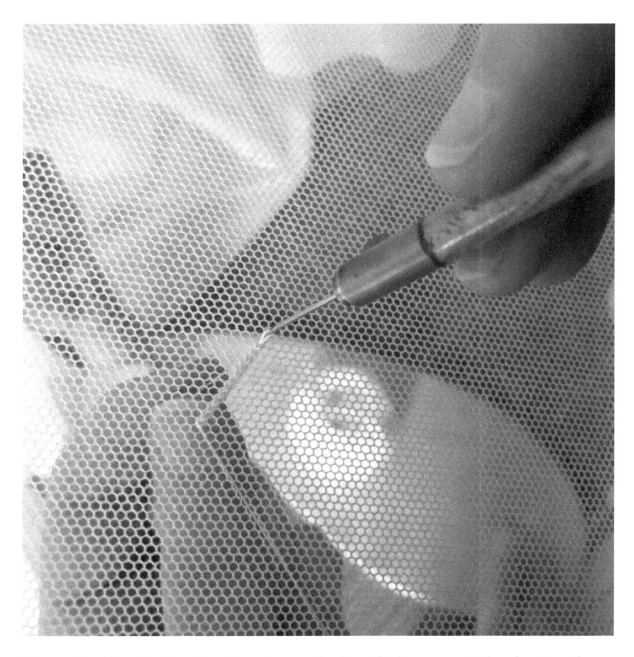

To make the distinctive tambour chain stitch, repeat the instructions above. a. Turn the hook in the direction you want to go. b. Hook the fabric with the hook. c. Wrap the thread around the hook and rotate it back towards the stitches. d. Pull the new thread loop through the fabric and the previous one.

As I move to the next stitch, I "un-rotate" the hook counterclockwise above the fabric, untwisting the thread loop.

If you drop the thread or accidentally take your hook out of the loop, don't panic. Put it back through the loop and into the next cell, and keep going. However, if you pull on the working thread before the hook has passed through the last loop, the entire work will unravel! If you see a mistake in your design and wish to go back and change it, simply pull the thread until the mistake is gone, reinsert your hook into the free loop, and continue as if nothing happened. But it's not so great if you've just gotten the hang of things and pull out all of the lovely stitches you've painstakingly linked together!

The most important thing to focus on once you've figured out how to make the stitch is tension. When the hoop tension is relaxed, the stitches will be loose and sloppy if you don't hold the thread taut enough with your off hand while embroidering. If you hold it too tightly, the stitches will be pulled too tight, causing the fabric to pucker. Concentrate on gliding the thread between your thumb and finger beneath the fabric. Consider the gentle, flexible tension you experience when removing the bobbin thread from a sewing machine.

Step 4: Complete the thread.

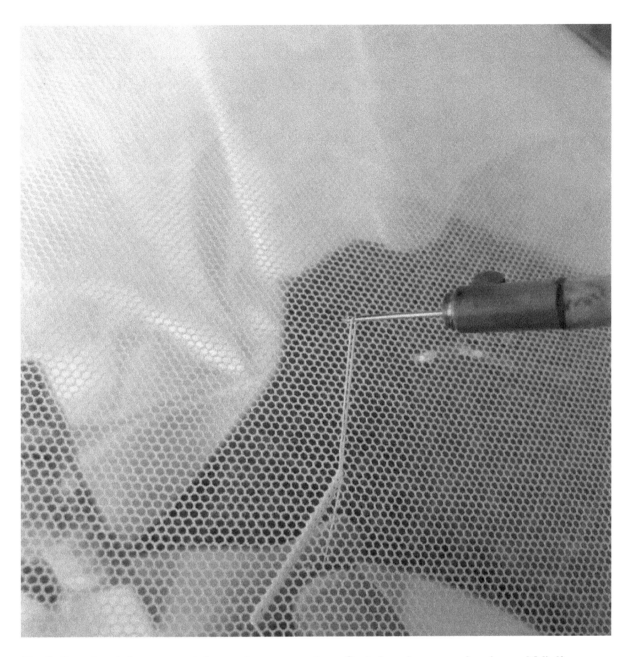

Pull the last loop out far when you've finished your design. While you turn the hoop and cut the working thread,

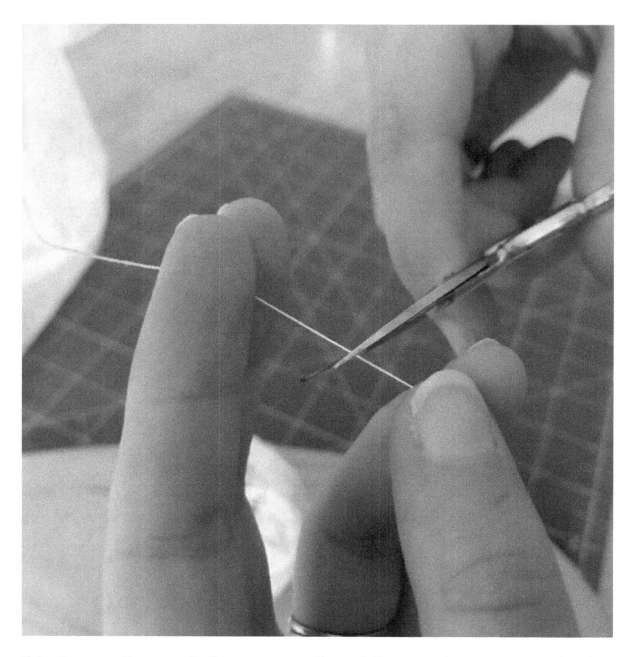

this keeps the work from unraveling. Lift your hoop and snip the working thread long enough to thread onto a needle.

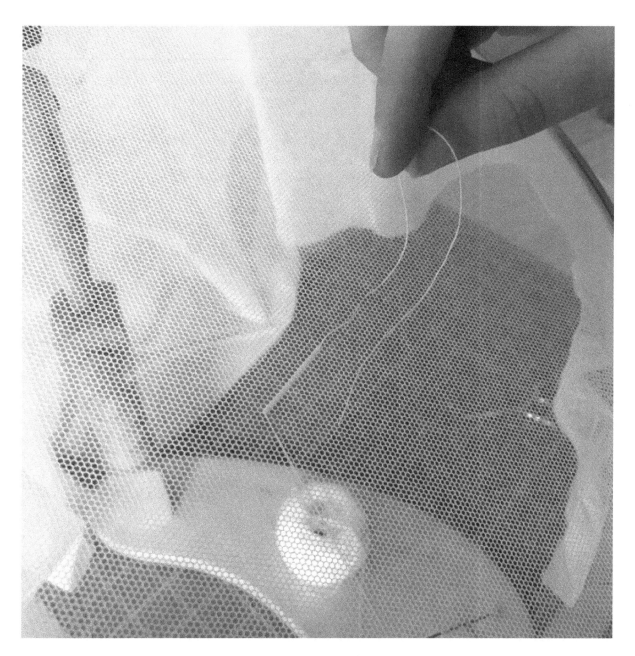

Pull your long loop so that the end of the snipped thread comes up through the top of the cloth. Flip your hoop back down so that the top side of the work is facing you. A thread end will now come up from the midst of the final stitch.

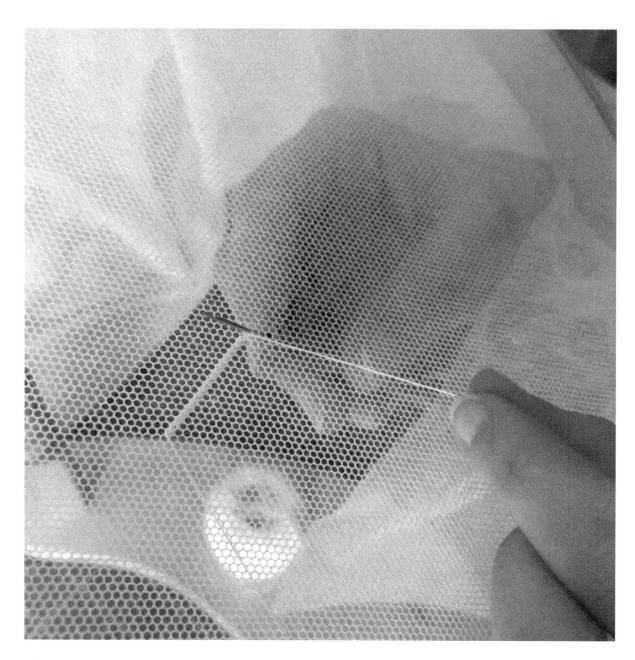

Hook up from the bottom of the cloth, but not through the stitch itself, in the same cell as your final stitch.

Wrap the end of your thread around the hook.

Pull the thread end all the way back to the wrong side of the work. This may appear insignificant, but it is all that is required to keep the stitches from unraveling.

Step 5: Finish by weaving in your ends.

This is something I cannot emphasize enough: do it as you go! How did I come to this conclusion? Because weaving in ends is boring but believe me when I say that weaving in ends is 10,000 times duller when you leave twenty or more until the conclusion of a project and then have to spend hours weaving them all in at once. Learn from my errors. Things' far more convenient to do it as you go. Fortunately, if you're adept at planning out a design path, you should be able to complete a single tambour motif, if not more, with only two ends of your thread. I'll show you how to skip from place to place in your design without cutting the thread in future tutorials, as well as other time-saving tips.

Finally, tying up loose ends.

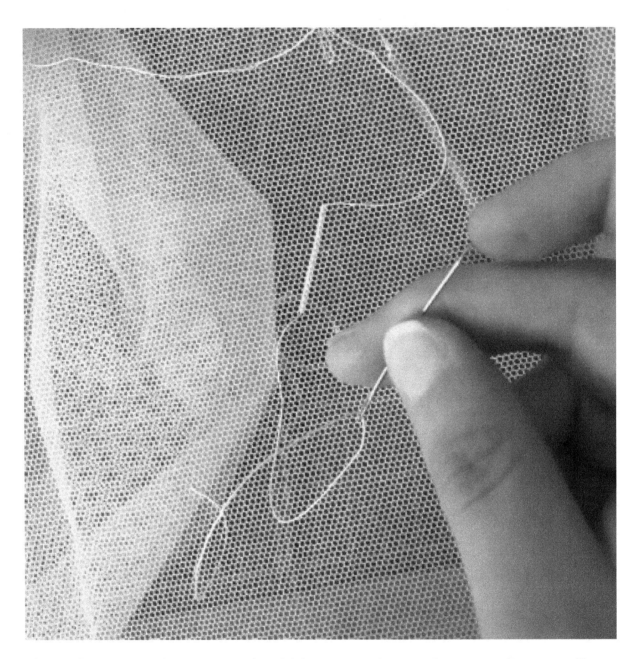

One of your trailing ends should be threaded onto a sewing needle.

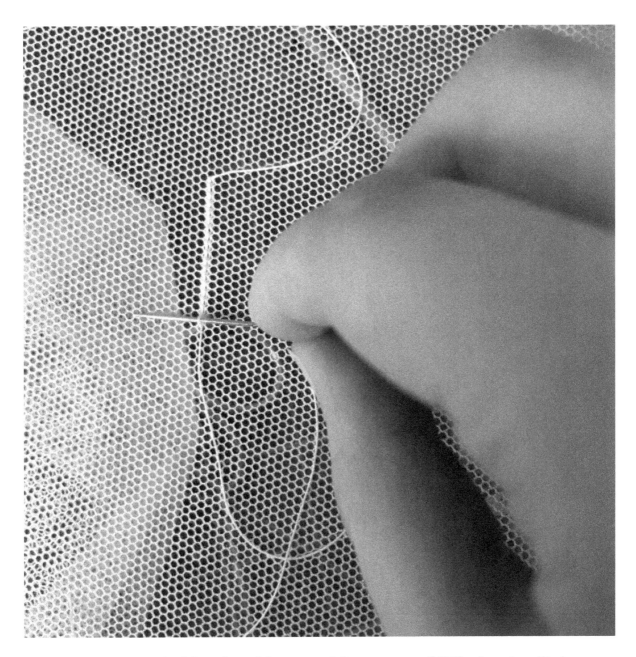

Your work's backside should resemble a row of little back stitches or machine stitches. Pull the needle through one of these stitches.

Pull the needle through the next "back-stitch" using the needle. Continue for at least an inch or two, or until you're confident that the thread is securely fastened. I barely did about a half inch to display because this line is so short. Make sure you don't pull these threads too tight or your chain stitch will pucker on the right side! You can also weave the ends through with your hook, but I find that using a needle is faster. Trim any surplus thread and repeat with any other loose ends.

Working from the back.

From the front, the chain stitch.

I've spent the last two weekends in Locust Grove doing one of my favorite things: dressing up and demonstrating needlework! I was performing tambour needlework for these demonstrations, which was a popular style of ornamentation from the mid-eighteenth century to the early nineteenth century, when it was eventually superseded by machine work and other hobbies. However, it has never fully disappeared and is still used to decorate haute apparel, particularly for bead and sequin work.

Tambour whitework, which creates a lovely lacy pattern on fine fabrics or net, was popular throughout the late 18th century and

Regency periods. It's a lot of fun and fulfilling to do, and it's a terrific demo because it moves faster than needle and thread embroidery, so even if people only watch me work for a few minutes, they can see a piece grow.

I'd been working on the first piece for quite some time before finishing it at the Gardener's Fair two weekends ago. It's a fichu embroidered with a pattern from Ackermann's Repository's August 1814 issue.

I was ecstatic to finally finish this work!

The second design dates back to March of 1814. I'm making two strips, each about 18 inches long, to use as sleeve cuff embellishment. I began working on these during the launch weekend of our Farm Distillery.

It's been a fantastic two weekends, but a peaceful weekend at home would be extremely welcome. For my Ravenclaw-inspired 1870s costume, I'll be wearing the bustle and petticoats once more!

www.ingramcontent.com/pod-product-compliance
Lightning Source LLC
LaVergne TN
LVHW080414121224
798954LV00029B/517